Labor Parties, 1827-1834

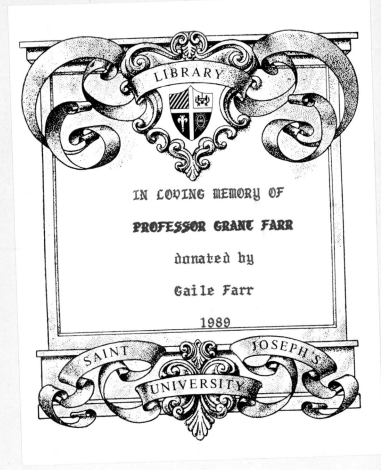

LABOR PARTIES
1827-1834

ALDEN WHITMAN

International Publishers, New York

CONTENTS

FOR H.K.W.—whose help, direct and indirect,
in the preparation of this booklet
has been enormous.

Introduction: Parties and Issues

The America of the 1820's and 1830's was huddled on the Eastern Seaboard. About 5,500,000 people lived in the North Atlantic states and 3,500,000 in the South Atlantic area while the remainder of the total population of 13,000,000 was about evenly divided between the North and South Central divisions. During the two decades, however, thousands of people were moving over the Appalachians and to the West, their journeys eased by the Erie Canal, improved turnpikes, and the new railroads.

Industrially and commercially, the country was centered in the big cities of the East, Philadelphia, New York, and Boston. The period of isolation following the War of 1812 was ended and increasing use of the steamship began to boom seaboard commerce with Europe. The factory system was gaining a foothold in Massachusetts and Rhode Island, spreading to New York and Pennsylvania. Textile "manufactories," employing mostly women and children, and iron-fabricating establishments dominated the factory scene.

In New York City in 1835 there were, for example, five textile factories, eleven iron works, nine tanneries and nineteen breweries and distilleries.[1] Organized trades claimed a membership of 11,500 in New York for the year 1834.[2]

The shift from handicraft to factory production was just beginning and as yet the main body of workers was journeymen and artisans, who were employed in small shops or by masters. Establishment of factories during the 'twenties was most marked in Massachusetts, where small cotton mills were expanded into corporate enterprises with millions of invested capital under the control of Boston financial circles.[3]

The dominance of New England in industrial development continued through 1830 and 1840, but estimates for the year 1850 reveal that in other sections more and more of the urban workers were becoming factory wage-earners. About 10 per cent of the total population of New England was employed in "manufactories" in 1850, while 6 per cent was so employed in the Middle Atlantic states—a considerable increase over 1830.[4]

During the 'twenties and 'thirties, wages were low and hours long, particularly in the factories. Through strike struggles, journeymen and artisans established a fairly general ten-hour day for themselves, but standard factory hours for all workers, women and children included, were from sunrise to sunset.[5]

Agitation for the ten-hour system continued through the entire period. Strikes were frequent and often bitter, both in the skilled trades and among factory operatives. The struggle for a shorter working day was one basis for the vigorous working-men's political parties. Along with lack of adequate educational facilities and opportunities, it constituted perhaps the most widespread grievance of the workers in the North and East. Trade union after trade union constantly made the ten-hour day its central demand. One of the provisions of the constitution of the New England Association of Farmers, Mechanics and Other Workingmen pledged the membership to the ten-hour day without any reduction in wages.

The third article of the Association's constitution reads:

"Each and every person that shall sign this constitution, except practical farmers, shall, so long as he may remain a member of the Association, stand pledged on his honor to labor no more than ten hours for one day, unless on the condition of receiving an extra compensation, at the rate of one-tenth part of a day's wages, for each extra hour he may labor, over and above the said ten hours per day. And any member offending against the provisions of this article, shall forthwith be expelled." [6]

Before 1827, the workers' movement was expressed in sporadic and isolated strikes, or "turn-outs," confined to single trades and carried through by hastily created organizations. They were developed in the face of harsh laws against combination and conspiracy, which were used to imprison strikers and terrorize the workers. The advantages of mutual aid, necessity for permanent organization and the desirability of independent political action were lessons which workers gained from their strike experiences.

Inequality between rich and poor, workers and big employers, was a characteristic feature of city life in the 1820's and 1830's. Leisure, learning, and comfort set apart the rich; hallmark of the great mass of wage earners was poverty, illiteracy, and squalor. Equal citizenship was impossible. The great promise of the American Revolution could not come true while such disparity existed on every hand. Overlong hours of work—"from sun to sun"—robbed the workingman of his leisure to consider public questions, while lack of public education left him without the requisite training and information with which to exercise the prerogatives of citizenship. He felt the oppression of such laws as those calling for imprisonment for debt, and of court decisions that branded his strikes for higher wages and better working hours as "conspiracies." Wildcat banking and fly-by-night business practices seemed further to fasten on the workingman a social arrangement whereby the "producing classes" (as the workers correctly thought of themselves) would be increasingly bereft of the fruits of their labor and their children after them would be condemned to a life of unremitting toil and poverty.

The policies of Jacksonianism were a continuation and enrichment of those of Jeffersonian democracy under different conditions. Jackson's administration was chiefly concerned with advancing democratic principles nationally, and left to the states and the municipalities the task of developing those principles locally. It was, therefore, logical for the workingmen, who supported Jackson and his national program, to organize labor parties in their own communities to put his policies into practice.

Jackson's own party, the Democrats, an outgrowth of Jefferson's Republicans, represented in the main the rising industrial class, the middle classes, and the producing (working) class. On the Eastern Seaboard, in New York, Philadelphia, and Boston, it was not a homogeneous political organization, but rather a coalition of progressive and forward-looking forces which rallied around Jackson's firm and vigorous democratic policies. In such a coalition it was natural for the workers to emerge as an independent group, otherwise their demands would have been ignored by those Democrats who assumed nominal leadership in the coalition. The labor parties, advancing the independent interests of the working men, thus strengthened popular support for Jackson and for his policies.

Dorothea Dix was drawing the attention of the public to the maltreatment of the insane and the imprisoned, and Horace Mann was pointing to the "little red schoolhouse" as something a little less attractive than a moderately well-kept pigsty. Women began, too, to insist that they were a part of humanity and held conventions to express their convictions. Slaves ran away from their masters, and working men were asserting their rights. The coonskin democracy of the Jacksonian era put old ideas to challenge.

The so-called aristocracy of property and intellect, which dominated Washington, ruled in the tradition of Alexander Hamilton. Aloof from the common people, the administrations before Jackson's time represented merchant and plantation capital. The voice of Daniel Webster and the Senate oratory of John Caldwell Calhoun were spent in the cause of special interests who regarded the development of the United States and its welfare as their particular prerogative. Entrenched in control of the economic, social, and political life of the nation since 1808, the slave owners of the South, the merchants and landed gentry of the North had begun to feel in the course of twenty years that they exercised a rule by divine right. The principles of the Declaration of Independence lay neglected for the poor and the uneducated. Yet, it was the poor and the unschooled which constituted the bulk of Andrew Jackson's support and which furnished the backbone of Jacksonian democracy.

The political changes which took place in the election of Jackson were surface symptoms of deeper agitation throughout the country. The Revolution, the Constitution with its Bill of Rights, and Thomas Jefferson had solved many of the problems of the young Republic, but such elemental problems of a democracy as education, land distribution, suffrage, union organization were left unsolved for the masses of people.

It was with those problems that people concerned themselves during the 1820's and the 1830's. The spirit of reform was in the air—reform in its literal sense of reshaping American society along the lines of equality and democracy.

This era of reform commenced with a revolt against the established religious practices of the dominant Protestant churches, and was particularly evident in the frontier regions. The largest and most significant revolt—Mormonism—had its beginning in Palmyra, New York, in 1819-20, but flourished in the "hinterland" of Ohio and Illinois, winning thousands of converts to its doctrines. Contrasted with the revival spirit of frontier religion was the Unitarian revolt against the established Congregationalism of New England. Although this revolt was conducted along highly intellectual lines and worded in terms of theology and dogma, the Unitarians represented a view of the world in which individual men and women were entitled equally to the fruits of industry and the products of the field. At least two prominent Unitarians, the Reverend Henry Colman in Massachusetts, and Orestes Brownson, in New York, actively participated in the workingmen's movement. Brownson's paper, the *Genesee Republican and Herald of Reform,* supported independent political action and advocated educational reforms.

Added to the movement for more democratic religious practices was widespread interest in Utopian schemes of various sorts. Utopianism, of course, was not new, but America was; and that newness encouraged such reformers as Robert Owen, the English Utopian Socialist, to believe that their experiments could succeed in a land free from the feudal hangovers of Europe.

Charles MacKay, in 1834, expressed in doggerel the positive hope of the Utopians when he wrote:

> *There's a good time coming, boys,*
> *A good time coming;*
> *The pen shall supersede the sword,*
> *And right, not might, shall be the lord*
> *In the good time coming.*
> *Worth, not birth, shall rule mankind*
> *And be acknowledged stronger;*
> *The proper impulse has been given—*
> *Wait a little longer.*

The goal of the Utopians of this period was summed up by an Englishman, who, looking longingly at the New World, wrote: "All shall have a good house to live in, with a garden back or front, just as the occupier likes; good clothing to keep him warm and to make him look respectable, and plenty of good food and drink to make him look and feel happy."

This statement is perhaps an oversimplification, since most Utopians were as interested in the methods of obtaining material comforts as they were in the comforts themselves. Thus, the Owenite colony, New Harmony, in Ohio and most other Utopian ventures were founded on principles of community co-operation. The Owenites pooled their resources, helped to work each other's land, co-operated in building essential public structures and the like.

The economic basis of American utopias was farming and small industry, while the social basis rested on schooling and education. The Owenites were convinced of the virtues of learning, and the school in the Ohio colony was something of a highwater mark in the history of American education, teaching the sciences and letters as well as the regular curriculum to both boys and girls.

The general tendency of the Utopians was to create a "simple" society, uncomplicated by the problems of a community dominated by factories and heavy industry. But cities in which the small artisan was characteristic were giving way before a growing tide of industrialization. It was this basic change in the country's economic life which foredoomed the Utopians, but which also encouraged their attempts to implant crude socialistic ideas. The change unsettled thousands of workers, depressed wages and living conditions and created new conditions of livelihood; it made them more receptive than ever to ideas and plans for a setup in which the harshness of industrial life under capitalism would be lessened.

Akin to Utopian ideas in its emphasis on agriculture were schemes for land reform which flourished during this period. The land reformers, most influential of whom was George Henry Evans, were city dwellers, whose interest in the problem of land distribution was twofold: They saw the public land (and the private, too) as a means of keeping wages in the cities at a high level; and they also believed that the land should be used to create a society of independent agricultural producers.

Reformers concerned with the public land (land owned by the United States and the state governments) argued that it should be set aside for sale at low prices to those who would actually settle and till it. The vast reservoir of land thus available, the reformers said, would both absorb immigrants from abroad (who were beginning to arrive in fairly large numbers during the 1830's), and would provide homesteads for city workers who were dissatisfied with wages and working conditions in the new factories. Since manufacturers would be faced with a situation in which workers could easily quit and trek to a homestead, they would be forced to pay "fair" wages to keep them at the factory benches.

"National Reform," under the guidance of Evans, made considerable headway, attracting support from workers' organizations and even from among some followers of Charles Fourier, French Utopian Socialist. Its theories of land reform also were influential in Congress, but they failed to create widespread response among most wage earners. Actually, it was not a simple transition to leave the city and set up on a farm. It appears that few workers were convinced of the virtues of land reform as a counterbalance to low wages, although they may have supported its opposition to land monopoly and to speculation in the public domain.[7]

Not all land reformers were concerned with the public domain; the presence of great estates led men like Thomas Skidmore to evolve plans for reform which would have broken up these estates, distributing the land to the tenants or giving title to the state governments.

The abolition of slavery was becoming more of a national issue during the 'twenties and 'thirties. Hitherto, agitation against slavery had been sporadic and directed less against the vicious

14

institution itself and more toward genteel schemes for colonization of Negroes in Africa. But now the movement for Abolition began, headed by William Lloyd Garrison and his *Liberator*. It was this group which pledged not to still its voices until the task of freeing the slaves and eradicating the institution of human bondage was accomplished.

Quite naturally the Northern and Eastern workingmen were concerned with slavery, not only on moral grounds, but also because it violated the rules of democracy. Support for Abolition was, however, slow to crystallize, and it was not before the 1840's that the trade unions became active supporters of the movement. Wages, working conditions, and the tasks of organization took precedence, although interest was never lacking.

Women's rights likewise was an issue of the times. Reformers like Frances Wright and Prudence Crandell fought for the right of their sex to education and for freedom from the restrictions which society imposed on them. Miss Wright and others like her believed that women were pushed into subordination and kept there, not because of any lack of ability, but because of outworn custom and prejudice.

Factory employers were willing enough to hire women to operate textile looms and other industrial machinery because it kept wages down, but these same employers were bitterly opposed to the doctrines of Frances Wright and insisted that women were born in order to let men and industry exploit them.

The measure of the times in which American labor first raised its political voice may be seen from the opposition to reform of all kinds from outraged conservatives.

The story of how the men from the frontier and poorer people from the East trampled through the White House with muddy boots at the inauguration of Jackson is a classic of textbook history. But when the United States rejected at the polls the aristocracy of property and intellect, this aristocracy cried out

15

in rage. That the common people might want to exercise the prerogative of democracy had been a constant fear since the days of Alexander Hamilton; that they now were doing so (in electing Jackson) drove the conservatives to a fury of rage.

The aristocratic newspapers turned their news and editorial columns against not only Jackson, but also against the reform movements. Frances Wright and her followers were pilloried in terms which today's *Chicago Tribune* reserves for President Roosevelt; education, land reform, Abolition, and the workers' movement were described as threats to "natural order," the Bible, and the foundations of the country.

Yet these shrieks were a measure of the tremendous changes that were taking place—changes in thinking and action, which affected not only the working people, but liberals and intellectuals as well. These changes were highlighted by the political movement of the workers.

Education and equality were intimately linked in the minds of the workers who resented the lack of school houses and opportunity for attendance, and the quality of instruction. Demand for "a general, equal and republican" system of education appeared in almost every expression of their political and economic belief. It was one of the cornerstones of the workers' movement despite disagreement over details. One expression, typical of many others, was formulated by a committee of Philadelphia workingmen in 1830, appointed by the Working Men's Party "to ascertain the state of public instruction in Pennsylvania, and to digest and propose such improvements in education as may be deemed essential to the intellectual and moral prosperity of the people."

"The original element of despotism," their report declared, "is a monopoly of talent, which consigns the multitude to comparative ignorance, and secures the balance of knowledge on the side of the rich and the rulers. If then the healthy existence of a free government be, as the committee believes, rooted in the will of the American people, it follows as a necessary consequence, of a government based on that will, that this monopoly should be broken up, and that the means of equal knowledge (the only security for equal liberty), should be rendered, by legal provision, the common property of all classes.

"In a republic, the people constitute the government, and by wielding its powers in accordance with the dictates, either of their intelligence or their ignorance; of their judgment or their caprices, are the makers and the rulers of their own good or evil destiny. . . .

"It appears, therefore, to the committee that there can be no real liberty without a wide diffusion of real intelligence; that the members of a republic should all be alike instructed in the nature and character of their equal rights and duties, as human beings, and as citizens; and that education, instead of being limited as in our public poor schools, to a simple acquaintance with words and cyphers, should tend, as far as possible, to the production of a just disposition, virtuous habits, and a rational self-governing character.

"When the committee contemplate their own condition, and that of the great mass of their fellow laborers; when they look around on the glaring inequalities of society, they are constrained to believe that until the means of equal instruction shall be equally secured to all, liberty is but an unmeaning word, and equality an empty shadow, whose substance to be realized must first be planted by an equal education and proper training in the minds and habits, in the manners, and in the feelings of the community." [8]

From this report, and others like it, it is evident that a public education system, free from taint of charity, was counted one of the first essentials of democracy. "The glaring inequalities of society" were abundantly summarized by the prevailing system of education, wherein the aristocrats' children went to fancy schools, and the workers' children were compelled to toil in the mills.

Two other factors helped to shape the workers' political movement. The right to vote for white men was generally spread over the North and East. Most property qualifications

17

for the franchise were removed in Massachusetts in 1820. New York liberalized the franchise in 1822. Pennsylvania suffrage rights extended to all those who paid any sort of a state or county tax. Secondly, cities were growing. In the decade of 1820, thirteen new cities acquired populations of over 8,000, and in 1840, 8.5 per cent of the country's population lived in cities.[9]

An extended franchise and population shift to the cities were part of the framework within which the movement developed. Its substance, however, lay in the determination of the workers to remedy their conditions, and to put life into the abstract phrases of democracy. This movement was a basic political expression, and it possessed that vitality which can come only from class feeling and class conviction.

LABOR PARTIES

In the early spring of 1827 a pamphlet circulated among the mechanics and workingmen of Philadelphia. It was addressed to the workers and spoke in their name; and its thinking suggests why a strike later in the year led to the establishment of a city central labor body and, shortly afterward, to a sizeable political movement.

It is, of course, no accident that Philadelphia, the largest and most advanced city in the Union, was the scene of this activity, for it was there, in 1791, that the first strike in American history took place, and many of the pioneer struggles of American labor occurred there prior to 1827. The workers of Philadelphia already possessed a tradition of militant struggle.

The pamphlet said in part:

"It is true in this favoured nation we enjoy the inestimable blessing of 'universal sufferage,' and constituting as we do, a very great majority, we *have the power* to choose our own legislators, but . . . this blessing . . . can be of no further benefit to us than we possess sufficient *knowledge* to make proper use of it. It will be an instrument of unlimited good to the great mass of people when they shall possess that degree of intelligence which will enable them to direct it *for their own benefit;* but at present this very blessing is suffered, through our lack of information, to be directed against our prosperity and welfare by individuals whose interest is at variance with ours." [10]

While the pamphlet did not specify political action it did

19

recommend establishment of a free press, libraries, reading rooms, and forums. One practical result was formation of the Mechanics' Library Company, which later published the *Mechanics' Free Press,* a weekly labor newspaper.

With the conclusion of the journeymen carpenters' strike for a ten-hour day, a movement got under way for some sort of central labor body in the city.

The central body instituted late in 1827 took the name, "Mechanics' Union of Trade Associations." Part of the preamble to its constitution, actually a statement of aims and purposes, is worth study, not only because it is the first statement of its kind in our history but also because it expresses with peculiar aptness the main political and economic issues of the day, and points to political action as the sole remedial solution for the class position of wage earners.

"Is it just," the preamble asks, "is it equitable that we should waste the energies of our minds and bodies, and be placed in a situation of such increasing exertion and servility as must necessarily, in time, render the benefits of our liberal institutions to us inaccessible and useless, in order that the products of our labor may be accumulated by a few into vast pernicious masses, calculated to prepare the minds of the possessors for the exercise of lawless rule and despotism, to overawe the meagre multitude, and fright away that shadow of freedom that still lingers among us? Are we to confer almost every blessing on society, never to be treated as freemen and equals, and never to be accounted worthy of an equivalent, in return for the products of our industry? Has the Being who created us given us existence only with the design of making it a curse and a burthen to us, while at the same time, he has conferred upon us a power with which ten-fold more of blessings can be created than it is possible for society either to enjoy or consume? No! at the present period, when wealth is so easily and abundantly created that the markets of the world are overflowing with it, and when in consequence thereof, and of the continual development and increase of Scientific power, the demand for human labour is gradually and continually diminish-

20

ing, it can not be necessary that we, or any portion of society should be subjected to perpetual slavery. But a ray of intelligence on this subject has gone forth through the working world, which the ignorance and injustice of oppressors, aided by the most powerful and opposing interests can not extinguish; and in consequence thereof, the day of human emancipation from haggard penury and incessant toil is already dawning. The spirit of freedom is diffusing itself through a wider circle of human intellect, it is expanding in the bosoms of the mass of mankind, and preparing them to cast off the yoke of oppression and servility, wherever and by whatever means it has been riveted upon them." [11]

Three significant ideas are touched upon in the preamble, which testify to the class consciousness of the workers. First, there is recognition of the fact that the capitalist class, "a few," expropriate the products of the workers' labor, and that this process, despite technological development, creates a system of wage slavery. Secondly, the state as controlled by the class of a few was seen as "the exercise of lawless rule and despotism." And, thirdly, there is the idea that the working class is that class in society which by its own activity will abolish the system of wage slavery, "expropriate the expropriators."

Self-assurance and militance are implicit throughout the preamble, which provided the Philadelphia political movement with its initial justification. Specific impetus for political action, however, may have been given in a review of the journeymen carpenters' strike, published in the *Mechanics' Free Press* (April 19, 1828). This urged that the City Council be petitioned to pass a law "making ten hours to constitute the standard day's work."

Discussing this suggestion and a number of other grievances at its meeting the following month, the Association decided to poll its constituent unions on the question of nominating candidates "to represent the interest of the working classes" in forthcoming elections for city council and state legislature. The

Association declared some of the worst evils visited upon society, especially the workers, were attributable to "an injudicious use, or criminal abuse of the elective franchise"; without adequate representation from the working class, ambitious and designing men were enabled to secure for themselves privileges and immunities belonging to all; and, thirdly, the election process (of 1828) tends to center control in the hands of a few.[12]

Significantly, the workers stated that as a class they have separate and independent interests, refuting those "special" historians and later day advocates of collaboration who claim that the class struggle is un-American. The fact is that the class struggle is as American as Plymouth Rock.

Response to the Association's poll came slowly as the various unions considered the proposal. The cordwainers (shoemakers) agreed, the hatters approved, and the carpenters' union, the main section of the Association, phrased its historic response in the following communication to the July meeting of the Association:

"At a very large and respectable meeting of Journeymen House Carpenters, held on Tuesday evening, July 1st, at the District Court Room, information was communicated by the Delegates, that the Mechanics' Union of Trade Associations is entering into measures for procuring a nomination of candidates for legislative and other public offices, who will support the interest of the working classes: an expression of opinion and sentiments on this subject having been called for, it was unanimously resolved that we entertain the most heartfelt satisfaction and approbation for the measures in contemplation by the said 'Mechanics' Union of Trade Associations,' and will use every exertion to carry the said measures into effect." [13]

The Association thereupon adopted a by-law, providing for nominations for the fall elections, with "a unanimity seldom witnessed in any of the political parties."[14]

Thus formally began the first venture of American workers into politics, in their own name, under their own leadership, and for their own benefit.

In order better to understand the situation in which the brave, new movement found itself, a word is in order to explain the electoral system of the times. Candidates for public office were nominated by convention and caucus meetings which were usually tightly controlled by machine politicians. Party membership involved only the loosest sort of attachment; there was no device for registration, as is the custom today. Property qualifications were general for all office holders, thus placing limits on those who might be nominated. Methods of voting were crude. At polling stations, voters were handed printed ballots (usually distinctively colored and shaped) by politicians from contending parties. Secrecy, under such circumstances, was virtually non-existent. Corruption was common and violence frequent, due to the bitterness with which machine politicians fought for petty graft.

From the outset, the party of the workingmen was obliged to fight for its existence. Professional politicians tried to break up its meetings either by hoodlum methods, or by packing the crowd with their own stalwarts. Either method was possible, for the new party apparently held meetings which were open to all comers.

The decision once taken, the city central body promptly (August, 1828), called four meetings in Philadelphia, urging attendance "without respect to party or sectional names." The body's action was summarized in an amazingly apt resolution which makes clear the workers' determination "henceforth to take the management of their own interests, as a class, into their own immediate keeping."

"Public meetings," the resolution asserted, "for the purpose of cooperation in the management of Elections have been sanctioned by long established custom; and are generally admitted to be consistent with the genius and character of popular governments; and in this country particularly it may be safely assumed that what is lawful in such cases for any portion of the community, cannot be less so for the Working Classes.

"It has also been the practice with men of similar views and pursuits to concentrate their strength and talents in order to secure to themselves the political guardianship of their peculiar interests. The advantages resulting from the exercise of this privilege have hitherto escaped notice of the majority of the working men, who, caught by the popular excitement of the day, follow in the wake of their wary leaders, and having mainly contributed to the elevation of their ambitious favourites, are doomed to sink again into their former insignificance. With such odds against them their influence as a body has assuredly declined, and with it their rights and privileges. But instructed at length by the experiences of past errors and misfortunes, and thoroughly convinced of their undoubted right to do so in such cases, the Mechanics and Working Men of the City and County of Philadelphia are determined henceforth to take the management of their own interests, as a class, into their own immediate keeping, and with this view propose the following resolutions preparatory to arrangements for the ensuing General Elections.

"RESOLVED, that this meeting recommend to the Mechanics & Working Men of the City to support only such men for the City Councils and State Legislature, as shall pledge themselves in their official capacity to support the interests and claims of the Working Classes.

"RESOLVED, that we pledge ourselves not to permit the measures growing out of this meeting to interfere with the arrangements of either of the contending parties in relation to the presidential question or congressional election.

"RESOLVED, unanimously, that four district meetings of the City be held as follows [list of places and dates], for the purpose of choosing delegates to form a ticket for Assembly and City Councils to be supported by Mechanics and Working Men at the next General Elections.

"RESOLVED, that this meeting respectfully recommend to the several district meetings to confine themselves in their choice of delegates entirely to Working Men." [15]

24

The district meetings culminated in nominating conventions where candidates for city and state office were selected. The Working Men's Ticket, as the roster of candidates was generally known, received its chief organized support from "committees of vigilance," appointed by the county nominating convention. Little is known today about these committees, but presumably they functioned as election committees, spreading propaganda, policing meetings, and assisting at the polls on election day.[16]

Although convention delegates were mostly workingmen, fear of economic reprisals through loss of jobs, and difficulty of meeting the property qualifications for office holding undoubtedly prevented nomination of wage earners as candidates. Instead, those nominated were asked to subscribe to the broad principles of the ticket, and "to support the interests and claims of the Working Classes." The fact that Working Men's candidates were placed on both the Jackson and the Federalist ballots lies in the circumstance that leaders of both parties sought to establish influence among the wage-earning population. The Federalist and Jackson designations were made *after,* not before, those of the Working Men.

Although some supporters of the ticket expected greater electoral results, the leaders of the movement saw the election as an impressive demonstration of strength on the part of a rather hastily improvised party. Commented the *Mechanics' Free Press,* on October 18, 1828: "The result has been equal to our most sanguine expectations; yet it may not be equally as satisfactory to our friends."

Leaders of the movement learned from the campaign that effective political action depends in large measure on organization, that genuine political activity is perhaps less concerned with mere campaigning and more with the day-to-day struggle to defend and secure the interests of one's adherents. Less than a month after the elections, therefore, the workers began the establishment of permanent political clubs in and around Philadelphia. Serving partly a social purpose, they were fundamentally centers of political and educational activity. Their stated function was to aid in the election of public officers and help secure "general diffusion of constitutional, legal, and political knowledge among the working people."[17]

The fruits of this enlightened activity appeared, in March, 1829, in the formation of a more stable, cohesive political organization under the name of the Republican Political Association of the Working Men of the City of Philadelphia. Formation of the Association followed a winter of intense political education and activity—in Southwark and Northern Liberties, Philadelphia's suburbs, as well as in the city proper. The workers seemed convinced of the necessity for centralizing their movement and giving it specific organizational form. The democracy of this step is shown in the fact that the Association itself did not make any nominations in the campaign of 1829; these were entrusted to the city and county conventions, delegates to which were chosen at ward meetings. Thus the club membership—the rank and file—exercised direct influence in the actual working of the Association.

The vigor and power of the Association alarmed the politicians of the major parties. Large campaign meetings during the fall of 1829, sizeable and sympathetic audiences, and increased interest in voting reflected a new force in the city's life, imperiling the rule of the merchant capitalists. Reacting characteristically to peaceful, democratic threats to their power, they attempted to rough-house meetings of the workers. In one instance, the city commissioners rounded up a goon squad of one hundred fifty men employed on public works to break up a meeting in one of the western wards. With admirable discipline, the meeting moved to another location and passed resolutions which denounced the city government for taking advantage of "the dependent situation of the labourers employed in the public service, by marshalling them for the avowed purpose of frustrating a meeting of freemen in the honest exercise of their rights." [18]

Politics by strong arm, however, merely emphasized the fact that both Democrats and Federalists were equally bankrupt. Neither had a labor record, or a labor program, although both insisted on paying elaborate lip-service to "the honest workingman." Beneath this hypocrisy, the Democratic Party sought to split the Association by provoking fruitless controversies, and raising the false issue of "radicalism." Federalists, on the other hand, tried to use the movement to bolster their flagging fortunes by placing Association candidates on their ticket. Nevertheless, the Association membership saw the dangers of old party influence in their councils. Many ward meetings passed resolutions warning convention delegates not to fuse with either Democrats or Federalists.[19]

So anxious was the Association membership to avoid old party commitments that they nominated candidates in advance of the others. Despite this precaution, the Federalists endorsed nine, and the Democrats three workers' candidates in the city, while in the county, the Federalists endorsed three assembly and senate candidates.

The campaign of 1829 was tense, with abundant evidence of pressure from employers to force their workers to vote the old party ticket. Despite intimidation, the Association tickets rolled up an increased vote over the previous year, and actually elected enough candidates to hold the balance of power in the city. Of the 54 workers' candidates in both city and county, 20 were elected, all of whom had received endorsement from either Federalists or Democrats.

Viewing the results, the *Mechanics' Free Press* (October 17, 1829) exulted: "The balance of power has at length got into the hands of the working people, where it properly belongs, and it will be used, in the future, for the *general* weal."

27

A feeling of solid accomplishment pervaded the ward clubs, where the real work of rolling up the vote—education and agitation—had been carried on. And the Association in Southwark, with an eye to the desirability of unrelenting political agitation, issued an "address," urging its members and supporters to "prepare for the coming season." "The objects we have in view," the statement declared, "are hallowed by the sympathy of patriotism—it is the finish of the glorious work of the Revolution." [20]

The Southwark workers struck one of the keynotes of the whole movement. To them, as to hundreds of thousands of the common people of the thirteen colonies, the Revolution was fought for equality, for the rights of man. The working class political movement of 1829 considered itself the continuator of the Revolution, of the struggle for day-to-day application of the rights of man, rights which were being thwarted by the power of aristocracy and money. The workers felt that their job was to set the country back on the true course which the Revolution had laid out. Lack of theoretical understanding, however, prevented leaders of the movement from understanding the limitations of the bourgeois-democratic revolution. These theories were developed later when Karl Marx and Frederick Engels developed Scientific Socialism.

Organization and education in the ranks of the movement continued through the winter and spring of 1829-30, resulting in strengthening the ward clubs. The city convention of 1830 revealed representation from fifteen wards.

Prior to this convention, however, organization spread to other Pennsylvania communities. Political associations were formed in Lancaster, Phillipsburg, Carlisle, and Pike Township. The Philadelphia associations were diligent in spreading information about their own actions, principles, and organizational structure. A special city and county convention, in fact, was called to extend the field of political activity. Its organizational proposals, however, were not particularly forceful, since the address urged merely election of "honest, fearless and capable agents." Just why the gathering did not call for formation of a statewide party is not known, but failure effectively to unite the parties that were springing up weakened the movement as a whole, and contributed to its decline in Philadelphia.[21]

Problems of organization occupied the membership during the 1830 campaign. The convention system of selecting candidates was relatively new; prior to 1830 they seem to have been composed of only a few delegates, but in that year, after much discussion, the party's county convention included 66 delegates. This was a deliberate effort to assure greater representation and more democratic control for the ward organizations.[22]

Aside from this problem, there was debate over the qualifications of candidates. Some of the rank and file thought that only workingmen should receive the Association designation, while others saw no objection to approving "tried friends" of the movement and the party. (In the election of 1829, the party nominated an employer of labor for State Senate, who was also endorsed by the Federalists. His defeat was widely attributed to the fact that, as an employer, he did not enjoy the confidence of the party membership.) Judging from resolutions of the ward clubs, and the county convention, a majority of the party favored nomination of workingmen only. The convention, for example, went on record urging support of only those men "who are engaged in productive pursuits," while the Allegheny County organization asserted that "however patriotic a man may appear to be, it is evident that none can so completely understand our interests, and that none will be so vigilant in protecting them as those, who in promoting the public welfare, most effectually secure their own." [23] These sentiments, class conscious in their expression and implication, found general approval throughout the party.

29

From its inception, the Philadelphia movement made it a practice to demand that its candidates publicly pledge support of the party and "the interests and claim of the working classes." This was an elementary safeguard against those who wanted to use the movement to advance their own careers, or those who might be tempted to turn their coats once in office. To the general pledge were later added pledges to support specific measures, and the ward clubs more than once instructed their delegates to vote for no candidate who would not make the necessary public avowal.

All progressive movements are at one time or another subjected to red-baiting. Enemies hope to split the ranks of the people, or to divert attention from the merits of program and tactics. The workingmen's movement was no exception. It was attacked by the conservative newspapers of the day as "anti-religious" and "agrarian." It was denounced as "workeyism" and accused of having connections with Frances Wright, the fiery exponent of women's rights and the abolition of slavery.

The workingmen, of course, were quick to deny any connection either with Miss Wright or with the principles of agrarianism (a theory of land redistribution, which would have penalized large property owners), and as a matter of fact branded as enemies of "our righteous cause" those who introduced religion or agrarianism into their political proceedings. "Infidelity" was another charge leveled at the party, presumably evoked because of Miss Wright's rationalist anti-clerical views. The "respectable" press was bent on arousing a lynch atmosphere against the workers who dared to assert their democratic rights.

In spite of denials, the press campaign must have cost some votes, for in the fall election, the workers lost the balance of power gained a year earlier. The Democrats carried both the city and the county, but the Association ticket received about

1,000 votes a candidate. In Northern Liberties, eight commissioners were elected.

Conservative newspapers, as might be expected, hailed the returns as "the death of workeyism," while the *Mechanics' Free Press* saw in them "a triumph of principle." Admitting a setback, this newspaper (October 16, 1830) placed the blame on the workers. "The result is another instance of the blindness of the working men to their own interests, and exhibits in bold and striking colours, how easily the public liberties may be endangered by the supineness of the people themselves."

So little is known of what occurred in the party during the winter and spring of 1830-31 that it is impossible to estimate the amount or quality of political activity. The *Mechanics' Free Press* contains little information, aside from continued emphasis in its columns on the necessity for political action. In its last issue, it urged "an immediate call" for a convention to consider political problems and lay plans for the next election.[24]

Zeal among the rank and file made possible city and county conventions later in the year, nomination of a ticket, and some activity in the clubs, but the zenith had been passed; election results were disappointing; no labor men were elected. This was the last election for which the Association named a slate of candidates, and in which the workingmen, as an organized body, were an independent and influential factor in politics.

NEW YORK CITY

A story in itself, the Philadelphia movement is unique in its lack of internal dissention. In New York City, on the other hand, dissention plagued the movement from the day it was organized.

There are, however, certain general points of program on which, it is worth noting, there was great unity, not only in New York, but wherever parties were organized. Along with powerfully worded demands for general, free education, there was a call for reform of banking methods and an end to monopoly. The banking system of the 1830's was especially haphazard, particularly in New York. There the legislature chartered banks without apparent restraint, and practically every one of them immediately proceeded to engage in imprudent speculation with depositors' funds. Numerous failures, along with a widespread practice of issuing bank notes on insufficient coverage, led to bitterness and dissatisfaction among the workers. Wages were commonly paid in bank notes (popularly known as paper money), whose value constantly fluctuated with the solvency or reputation of the bank of issue. Because of this, merchants and trades people took bank notes only at a discount, and hence the workers' purchasing power varied from week to week, and even from day to day. Credit was hard to get. In almost every city, workingmen sought the abolition of bank notes, and the payment of wages in specie.

Other significant demands were for abolition of imprisonment for debt, the auction system, enactment of a suitable mechanics' lien law, and opposition to public charity.[25]

About twenty demands were raised by the various workers' parties, including New York. Added to those already mentioned were: abolition of the tariff, lotteries, prison labor; repeal of conspiracy laws against trade unions; and less manufacture of "ardent spirits." Practically all of these demands were fought by the old political parties during the lifetime of the workers' movement. Presumably, as a bid for support, some of them were "taken over," or adopted later, including the demand for abolition of debt imprisonment and the enactment of a mechanics' lien law.

Chief medium for the spreading of workingmen's ideas was the newspapers. And as the movement grew there emerged a working class press. In New York City, each dissident faction established its own press, counting it an essential tactic. In all, about fifty newspapers were established in cities where the movement took hold; these were devoted to news and articles on political subjects, and editorial agitation for the movement.[26]

Agrarianism and education were the issues causing factional strife in New York. A leader of the movement when it emerged from a struggle against attempts to extend the working day from 10 to 11 hours, Thomas Skidmore propounded agrarianism as a solution to the workers' conditions.

Skidmore's theory traced the poverty and insecurity of the great mass of the population to the unequal distribution of landed property. He urged equal division of the land of New York State through a complicated plan involving a State Constitutional Convention, abolition of debts and property claims, and redistribution. A statement which Skidmore drew up for the Working Men's Party asserted that before the workers could be saved from "present evils," a revolution must take place "such as shall leave behind it no trace of that government which has denied to every human being an equal amount of property on arriving at the age of maturity, and previous thereto, equal food, clothing and instruction at public expense."[27]

Proposals for land reform, such as that of Skidmore, have been frequent in the course of our history. About twenty years after Skidmore's plan, another movement, similar in its fundamental ideas, arose to claim the attention of the workers. An American Socialist, Hermann Kriege, anxious to discover the working class attitude toward it, wrote to Karl Marx in 1846 for advice. Marx analyzed the proposal for land redistribution as a petty-bourgeois movement, but urged support of it, because it was directed at property in general. Lenin's comment adds further enlightenment, and is particularly interesting to us in evaluating the attitude of the New York workers to Skidmore's plan.

". . . Marx does not simply 'repudiate' this petty-bourgeois move-

33

ment, does not dogmatically ignore it, for fear, as is characteristic of many text jugglers, of soiling his hands by contact with petty-bourgeois democracy. While mercilessly ridiculing the absurdity of the ideological integument of the movement, Marx strives in a sober, materialistic manner to determine its *real* historical content, the consequences which must inevitably follow from it because of objective conditions, regardless of the will and consciousness, the dreams and theories, of various individuals. Marx, therefore, does not condemn, but fully approves of communists supporting the movement. Adopting the dialectical standpoint, *i.e.,* examining the movement from every side, taking into account both the past and the future, Marx notes the revolutionary aspect of the attack on private property in land. Marx recognizes the petty-bourgeois movement as a peculiar initial form of the proletarian, communist movement. You will not achieve what you dream of by means of this [petty-bourgeois] movement, says Marx to Kriege; instead of fraternity, you will get petty-bourgeois isolation; . . . instead of inalienable peasant allotments, the land will be drawn into commerce; instead of a blow at the grabbing speculators, the basis for capitalist development will be expanded. But the capitalist evil you are vainly trying to avoid is historically good, for it will frightfully accelerate social development and bring ever so much nearer new and higher forms of the communist movement. A blow struck at landed property will facilitate further blows at property in general, which are inevitable." [28]

Unequipped with a full theoretical grasp of the real meaning of Skidmore's scheme and seeing in it no immediate solution to their problems as city wage workers, the New York Working Men's Party disavowed it. Upon its rejection, Skidmore founded his own organization and continued to carry on agitation for land reform.[29]

Education was another source of friction and dispute. Robert Dale Owen, son of the Utopian Socialist, and in his own right an influential humanitarian, was closely associated with the founding of the New York Working Men's Party. Agreeing with the need for independent political action, he saw in it a vehicle to advance his own plan for improving the educational system of the state. Owen's plan involved establishment of state boarding schools, open to the rich and poor alike, where children would be educated, clothed and fed at public expense until they reached maturity. Because public authorities would assume complete control of the children during this period, the plan was commonly known as "State guardianship."

Owen's conception of general education differed sharply with that of other members of the Working Men's Party, who wanted to improve the so-called day or literary schools by enlarging the curriculum, improving the standard of instruction, and opening the classroom doors to the sons of the poor. (Schooling for girls was not then considered genteel, private instruction being the rule where it could be afforded.) Partisans of Owen saw few advantages in perpetuating day schools. "Is that education the best," they asked, "by which children spend five or six hours out of the twenty-four in the streets, learning rudeness, impertinent language, vulgar manners and vicious habits? Will any advantages in school compensate for the disadvantages out of it?" [30]

In addition to the fact that day schools exercised no control over "after hours," there was this objection: "But even if none of these reasons existed, how is the poor laborer or the poor widow to keep her children at day school, until they have received an education equal to that of their rich neighbors?" [31]

In the spirit of democracy, therefore, Owen proposed "state guardianship [which] shall provide for all children, at all times, receiving them at the earliest age their parents choose to entrust them to the national care; feeding, clothing and educating them to the age of maturity." [32]

Dissension over this plan, cutting deeper than that over agrarianism, also resulted in the formation of a separate workers' party and contributed to the fatal splitting of the whole movement in New York.

35

Formation of the party in the spring of 1829 followed two mass protest meetings called by "mechanics and others" (presumably journeymen) to quash efforts to lengthen the working day. The second meeting, attended by over five thousand workers, named a "Committee of Fifty" as a continuations group to consider further action in the interests of the workingmen. Meeting during the summer and early fall of that year, the committee devised a report which recommended establishment of an independent political party. Made public at a meeting on October 19, 1829, it reflected very strongly the agrarian thinking of Skidmore, who was one of the committee leaders.

In two successive meetings, candidates for state assembly and senate were chosen, all of whom, except the two Senatorial nominees, ran solely on the workingmen's ticket. While the method of selection was rough and ready (partly because of inexperience and partly because use of the convention methods would have left no time for a campaign), the assembly ticket made clear the reliance which the new party placed on its own membership. The ticket consisted of two machinists, two carpenters, a printer, a brass founder, a whitesmith, a painter, a green grocer and a physician. Predominance of skilled artisans is characteristic; they constituted the party's backbone from the beginning, and it was their problems which helped shape the movement's program.[33]

Adoption of a ticket met with immediate response from organized trades. Although only a week elapsed between nominations and elections, at least three trades, among them the painters' union, endorsed the new party. The *Working Man's Advocate,* New York counterpart of the *Mechanics' Free Press,* began to appear on October 31—in such haste that its prospectus was printed as part of the first number. Mirroring the prevailing optimism and the spirit of hope among the workers, its leading editorial declared, "The working classes have taken the field, and never will they give up the contest till the power that oppresses them is annihilated."

36

The new party polled over 6,000 out of 21,000 votes, and elected Ebenezer Ford to the Assembly. The results were remarkable because they were achieved without organization on a platform consisting solely of generalities. Workers' indignation over the inequalities of the times, their distrust of the old parties and their desire to find a way out of the restrictions of a developing capitalist economy, all account for this successful start. Surveying the returns, the *Working Man's Advocate* of November 7, 1829, declared:

> "The result has proved beyond our most sanguine expectations, favourable to our cause . . . the cause of the people. . . . In spite of the opposition of most of the city papers, and without *one* in our favour—in spite of the immense *banking* influence, which was especially invoked when it was ascertained that we had a prospect of success, we have at least six thousand votes, out of twenty-one thousand, while we had four other tickets to contend with. . . . We have done more than reasonably could be expected at this election. We have, to a certainty, paved the way to future victory."

To sustain their success, it was necessary for the workers to organize a political party. Losing no time, a meeting of "mechanics and other workingmen," called within a few days of election, instructed the Committee of Fifty to devise an organizational plan. Two schemes were advanced, one which would organize the party on a ward basis, and another which would establish general, city-wide meetings as the basic organizational form. The general meeting plan was Skidmore's suggestion. He argued that it was "simple" and democratic, whereas the ward plan would open the party to infiltration by its foes. Effective control, of course, would remain in the hands of the Committee of Fifty, or some similar executive body, whose responsibility to the rank and file would be difficult to define. The ward plan, on the other hand, would help give the party a foothold in the neighborhoods where the workers lived, organizing clubs and centers of political agitation and education.

Skidmore's proposal, adopted by the committee, met with immediate resistance from the rank and file, who proceeded to organize ward meetings, endorsing the ward plan of organization. In eight out of fourteen wards impromptu meetings assembled and elected a committee of twenty-five, vested with power to elect five of their number to a city-wide general executive body.

Back of these actions were three factors. First, the rank and file were enthusiastic about the prospects for their party. Then, there was considerable dissatisfaction with Skidmore's agrarian program, which had been bestowed upon the infant party without much discussion. Workingmen suspected that the general meeting scheme would strengthen Skidmore's control over the party apparatus. Finally, they believed that the success of the Philadelphia organization lay in district and ward clubs.

This opposition resulted in dissolution of the Committee of Fifty, and adoption of the ward organizational plan.

The workingmen also made it understood that "the mechanics and workingmen and those friendly to their interests, hold the right of individuals both as to property and religion, as sacred as the instrument that declared our independence." [34]

Resolutions were passed at the meeting where this plan was adopted denouncing imprisonment for debt, banks and bank notes, and the militia system; enactment of a suitable lien law was also asked. Bidding for sympathy and understanding of their demands by the farmers, the meeting asked for support from "the mechanics of the country."

Education received only general treatment.

"Another object for which we contend," stated the address of the meeting, " . . . is the appropriation of our public funds to a reasonable extent, for the purposes of education, upon a system that shall enable all before the age of twenty-one to acquire a competent knowledge of the language of their country, arithmetic, geography, history, natural philosophy, geometry and chemistry, as applied to the arts. A system that shall unite under the same roof the children of the poor man and the rich, the widow's charge and the orphan, where the road to distinctions shall be superior industry, virtue and acquirements, without reference to descent."

Clearly a compromise, this statement served the politics of the moment. It did not serve to allay the demands of the guardianship group, although it did make possible initial organizational steps, such as formation of the General Executive Committee, formally instituted on January 15. It held thereafter weekly meetings, appointing sub-committees to investigate and report on imprisonment for debt, banking and education.[35]

Composition of the committee reveals the general character of the party, emphasizing that its base failed to include factory workers and women, who were being driven into industry in large numbers. Of the seventy members, six did not give their occupation; five were grocers; two, merchant tailors; one each an oil merchant, teacher, farmer, and broker. The remaining forty-two members were distributed as follows: eleven carpenters, four cabinet makers, four black and whitesmiths, three masons, three painters, two boat builders, two chair makers, two paper stainers, two brass-founders, two pianoforte makers, and one each of the following: manufacturer of fancy goods, stoneware manufacturer, silver plater, umbrella maker, window-blind maker, turner, portable furnace maker, cartman, tailor, tin-plate worker, porter house keeper, ship joiner, musical instrument maker, sash maker, and Morocco dresser. Noah Cook listed himself as "a working man," although the New York City directory three years later gave his occupation as "forwarding merchant."

While not explicit, it may be assumed that the committeemen were mostly journeymen. In fact the *Advocate* asserted that "if the occupations are given correctly by the individuals themselves, there is but one of the committee who is not a working man." [36]

From the first meeting of the committee, the division over education was apparent. Chairmanship of the body was decided with that in mind, and when Henry Guyon, an anti-Owenite, was elected, disapproval of state guardianship by a majority of the committee was a foregone conclusion.

The majority proposal, drawn up by Guyon, attacked Owen's plan as "a specious attempt insidiously to palm upon the committee and the great body of the working classes the doctrines of infidelity." [37]

Guyon's report, indeed, consisted largely of attack, submitting no proposal on behalf of the sub-committee on education other than a general one "for a republican system of education." A more elaborate plan was promised "in due time," but if ever devised, it was never made public.

Despite the negative approach to state guardianship, the majority had a real point in its condemnation of Owen's extra-party activities. Previous to the 1829 election Owen had formed an "Association for the Protection of Industry and for the Promotion of National Education." Trade unions were later circularized in its name. The *Daily Sentinel,* appearing February 15, 1830, and advocating guardianship, was largely backed by Owen. Neither of these activities served to promote party harmony, or focus the attention of workers on the central problems which confronted them.

But whatever the merits of his plan, Owen was not its own best exponent in the workingmen's movement. His anti-religious views invited hostility, but more important, his chief interest did not lie in organizing independent class action. While he subscribed to the humanitarian demands for abolition of imprisonment for debt and the like, he tragically failed to relate his own scheme to the movement as a whole. He was, therefore, willing to splinter the party, rather than work to build it into an effective instrument of class protest against the emerging capitalist system.

The majority was, on the other hand, not without its own shortcomings. Using the charge of "infidelity" to discount Owen, they fell into the trap of baiting one of their own number with the same charge which the conservative and monied interests were using against the movement as a whole. If Guyon and his friends felt that they were cleansing the party by charging Owen with "infidelity," they were mistaken, for they succeeded only in weakening the movement and in retarding its growth.

With adoption of the equivocal majority report, a bitter struggle for party control ensued from which neither group emerged secure in the allegiance of the workers. Each began to hold ward meetings, and soon there were two General Executives, each claiming to be the "original" party.[38]

Neither Owen nor Guyon were able to see beyond their differences, and animosities kept the party split.

NEW YORK STATE

The inherent power of the movement and the readiness of the workers to strike out for themselves is demonstrated by the spread of action throughout New York State where workingmen's parties developed during 1830 and '31. Albany, Salina (now Syracuse), Troy, Rochester, Utica, and other cities were centers of activity.[39]

Adopting programs similar to those already described, "the Farmers, Mechanics and Workingmen" participated in the spring elections of 1830, winning majorities in Syracuse, Troy, and Albany. Soon parties were in evidence all over the state, bursting with restless energy and confident of the justice of their cause. These parties gave substance to a suggestion made in the *Advocate* that a statewide convention of workers' parties was necessary. Coming before the split in the city party was actually confirmed, Evans, editor of *Advocate,* wrote in his newspaper on April 17, 1830, that a state convention would be worthwhile "not so much on account of the prospect of electing . . . officers . . . as for the facility it would afford us of disseminating a correct knowledge of the principles upon which the working men have organized throughout the state."

The *Advocate* was barely off the press when word came from Albany that a meeting of "farmer, mechanics and workingmen, and those friendly to their interests" had offhand nominated a candidate for governor, a certain General Erastus Root. A Tammany Democrat, and not previously identified with the workers' movement, General Root was a complete surprise. The meeting also directed the Albany party executive to arrange for a state convention to name a candidate for lieutenant-governor.

Late in July, the call went out and when the convention was called to order at the Syracuse Court House on August 25, 78 delegates from thirteen counties registered. Contending delegations from the Owen and the Guyon groups brought the city split to the convention floor where the delegates refused to seat the state guardianshipites. The convention confirmed the nomination of General Root and selected as his running mate General Nathaniel Pitcher. The platform, as embodied in the address and resolution, was a lukewarm affair, pledging loyalty to "republican principles," and advocating increased public education and the abolition of imprisonment for debt.

Convention weaknesses were obvious. None of the tasks of party organization or program was clarified or strengthened, and the nominees themselves, as the *Advocate* pointed out, in its September 4 issue, were "decided party men." The platform, too, failed to emphasize "the *rise* of the Working Men's cause."

The convention's failure to maintain labor's independent role in politics was soon apparent. Both nominees refused to run about two weeks before the election, and the party was left without candidates.

Owen's group, however, did make its own nominations shortly after the Syracuse Convention. Its men were said not to be "hacknied in the trade of politics," and at least they stood by their nominations. The group, moreover, chose congressional candidates in New York City and for the state legislature.

Skidmore's agrarian splinter group likewise had a ticket in the field. Thus, there were three workmen's tickets in the field, competing with the Democrats and the anti-Masons, with whom the remnants of the Federalist Party were, in the main, allied. The Syracuse group had candidates for Congress and for local office in various parts of the state. But defection of General Root and the indecisiveness of the convention smothered enthusiasm. The only victory was in Albany where thirteen out of twenty aldermen were elected. Statewide, of course, the workingmen were badly beaten.

During its troubled existence, the Working Men's Party threw the fear of loss of class position into the conservative elements of the community. As always more adept at smearing the workers than telling the truth about them, newspapers of the day did their best. "Mob," "rabble," "dirty shirt party," "tag, rag and bobtail," "workeyism," "ring-streaked and speckled rabble" were a few of the terms applied to the workers.

Of the demands which the party raised, great emphasis was placed on correction of the banking system; it was this that caused the greatest uproar in the newspapers, for the banks were the sacred cows of the rich.

A bit of doggerel sums up the workers' attitude toward the banks and toward bank notes. Entitled *The Idler and the Workers,* it reads:

Of paper coin, how vast the power!

It makes or breaks us in an hour,
And probably a beggar's shirt,
If finely ground, and freed of dirt,
Then re-compress'd, by hand or hopper,
And printed on with a plate of copper,
Might raise ten "Idlers" to renoun,
And tumble fifty "Workers" down.

Two solid accomplishments may be traced to the New York movement: abolition of imprisonment for debts in 1831 and enactment of a partial mechanics' lien law in 1832. Both were results of the workers' own activities.

NEW ENGLAND AND DELAWARE

"The poor have no laws; the laws are made by the rich and of course *for* the rich." This statement, part of an address by the Association of Working People of New Castle County, Delaware, in 1829, is typical of the vitality of the workers' movements outside of New York and Philadelphia. The same address urged "union among the working people," counseling them "to arise in their strength in support of their own interests." [40]

Reaching its zenith in 1830, the sturdy Delaware movement captured thirteen out of eighteen of the chartered officers of the borough of Wilmington. Despite its short existence, this movement seems to have been the only one to consider enfranchisement of women. Although such a step may have occurred to those in other sections as a plausible part of the general concept of equality, no public action was taken.

"We apprehend," asserted the address of the New Castle County workers in 1831, "that it would be no easy task, at this more advanced part of the march of the mind, to maintain the ground that was assumed, in excluding females from the right of voting at the

44

polls. This interesting portion of the community comprise a fair moiety of our population. Wherefore should they be denied the immunities of free men? Does anyone deem that their interference in public affairs would be prejudicial to the general interests? Or would we pretend to measure their capabilities for judging correctly, in relation to self-government? Let us reflect that it has not been considered commendable to give their attention to these subjects. Let data be found, before an attempt is made to calculate the extent and utility of their influence, or the salutory effect of their taking part in that in which they have, or ought to have an equal interest." [41]

Less enlightened, however, was the Association's suggestion to confine suffrage to "free white persons."

Starting in Connecticut, the workers' political movement spread throughout New England to Maine, Vermont, Massachusetts, and Rhode Island, and into the southern part of New Hampshire. The seacoast town of New London, Connecticut, where shipbuilding employed many workers, was the center of New England activity before it shifted to Boston with the formation of the New England Association of Farmers, Mechanics and Other Working Men, in 1831 and 1832.

These scattered parties were a prelude to the Association, which grew out of a meeting in Providence, Rhode Island, in December, 1831. (For a complete list of cities where workers' movements were established, see Appendix, page 63.) The basic grievance which the Association was formed to eliminate was "the daylight to dark" working day. The ten-hour day for mechanics was won less quickly in New England than in Philadelphia and New York, due to the greater degree of industrialization in New England. There, mill owners feared that the "contagion of shorter hours" would spread to factory workers, and acted, therefore, in support of efforts to crush strikes of carpenters, masons and ship carpenters for the ten-hour day. [42]

The ten-hour movement, however, had political ramifications, which the Association helped to develop as it branched out into independent political action. As a body, it did not engage in politics, although its constituent bodies in various cities, and especially in Massachusetts, not only prepared and circulated petitions to state legislatures, but put tickets into the field.

The Association differed in at least three fundamental respects from the Philadelphia and New York movements. First, it made an effort to appeal to the farmers, declaring that "there is an indissoluble connection between the interests of the cultivator of the soil, and the mechanics and every class of laborers." [43] The common enemy was "the idle, avaricious and aristocratic" classes.

Secondly, the Association recognized the necessity of bringing the factory operative within the orbit of the workers' movement. These workers, women and children for the most part, who constituted the "manufacturing population," had a common bond with other producers. On several occasions, conventions of the Association discussed particular problems of factory workers, and there was continuing consideration of their condition with relation to the large problem of education. Little or no direct organizational work among factory workers, however, appears to have been done, if one can judge from the complaint of a New Haven delegate to the 1833 convention, on the absence of delegates from factory villages. This delegate was of the opinion that factory workers were "already subdued to the bidding of employers," and asserted that the farmers and mechanics were "the last hope of the American people." [44]

Thirdly, the Association sought to extend itself organizationally, through bodies and societies, in the towns and villages of New England. It sought to bring all producers together, accustom them to joint action, to give their grievances and their remedial efforts organizational form. In this respect, as well as in those just enumerated, it marked a higher level of development than the Philadelphia and New York parties.

In all the Association held four conventions, two in 1832 and

46

one in 1833 and in 1834. The first convention did little more than devise a constitution for the Association, providing among other things for a treasury, and for a membership pledge to work only a ten-hour day. Prior to the second convention in September 1832, Association branches were established in Boston, Lowell, New Bedford, and other places. With this in mind, the delegates from five states (most of whom were informally chosen because of the lack of formal organizations in their communities), proposed "the organization of the Working Men in every town and county of New England," establishment of state central committees, and suggested "the expediency of a National Convention, to meet in some central part of the Union, representing the workingmen of the United States." [45]

While these proposals were not carried out, it is interesting to note that advanced sections of the workers' movement were thinking in terms of national organization, and clearly saw the practicability of strong organizational units, reflecting the needs of the workers.

The third convention, held in Boston in October 1833, was composed of about 25 delegates from four states. Here, there was discussion and committee reports on imprisonment for debt, education, child labor in factories, and "the condition of working women in this country." The banking system was also a topic for animated debate. These committees recommended that the various state delegations prepare petitions for their own legislatures on the various subjects. The convention took an important step forward when, by resolution, it urged "the Farmers, Mechanics, and Working Men of every description . . . to form themselves into Societies . . . with a view to the establishment of Trades Unions. . . ." [46]

National organization was likewise endorsed with the implied understanding that it might result in political action. Entrance into politics through a party apparatus was in the air; the con-

47

vention president mentioned it at length, and a committee strongly endorsed the idea of "recourse to the Ballot Box" as a means of redressing the wrongs of the producing class. In addition, the independent political attitude of Samuel C. Allen in declining to be an old party candidate for state office was heartily approved, leading to his nomination as governor by the Association in that year.

The Association made little headway after this convention. It remains, however, the most advanced, generally speaking, of all of the workers' organizations of the period, if only for its clear and consistent grasp of the need for trade union organization and for bringing factory workers into the organized labor movement. In this, its thinking and planning took into account the trend of industrial development which the country was to follow.

CONCLUSIONS

Various reasons have been assigned for the decline and disappearance of the early labor parties. Miss Helen L. Sumner, in her discussion of the Philadelphia Association in Commons' *History of Labour in the United States,* believes that a "combination of purely political causes" is responsible. She suggests the workers' "inability" to play the game of political intrigue coupled with the adeptness of old-line politicians. The "distractions" of the Presidential campaign of 1832 were also a factor, Miss Sumner claims, together with a gubernatorial campaign in 1832, and a cholera epidemic which took a huge toll in the Philadelphia working class districts.[47]

Other factors, however, must be considered, for it is not reasonable to suppose that either a Presidential election or narrow "political" causes would destroy a movement which had achieved the maturity and the successes of that in Philadelphia. It is true that the Association refrained from engaging in national politics to any great extent, because it did not feel equipped to function on a national scale. This self-imposed limitation contributed to the weakness of the party at a critical time, but it was not decisive.

Weaknesses inherent in the various movements caused their failure. These weaknesses had their basic origin in the state of development of capitalist society. It must be remembered, in the first place, that class lines in the United States were unstable. Differences between rich and poor were obvious, but there was a good deal of passing from moderate poverty to moderate wealth. Journeymen could still hope to be masters one day, and many

49

actually did succeed in establishing their own businesses.

Preponderant support for the "workingmen's ticket" came from the journeymen and those engaged in skilled trades. Significant changes in the mode of production, which were to alter the future of both labor and capital, were taking place at this time. Factories were springing up as merchant capital was being.transformed into industrial capital. This transformation was of immediate benefit to new industrial employers, who were able to take advantage of the relatively weak and isolated workers.

In political and as well in "pure" trade union action it might at first glance be expected that the factory workers, the new industrial proletariat, would have seized the initiative. But factory workers, a great percentage of whom were women and children, were as yet a disorganized mass with no unions to protect them. In contrast to factory "operatives," the craftsmen had their unions and guilds. These organizations provided an essential spirit of solidarity; they helped imbue the workers with a sense of the worth and dignity of human labor.

Their security and status threatened by the changing mode of production, skilled craftsmen fought hard against both merchant and industrial capital. It was a fatal mistake, however, that the parties paid little or no attention to the factory workers; they did not encourage trade union organization among them, agitate for women's rights or, in general, develop political understanding. They took no action on the fact that low factory wages and long hours and brutal exploitation lowered their own standards of work and living. Indeed, one of the important weaknesses of the workers' movement was lack of a trade union program even for the journeymen. Nowhere in its addresses or publications does one find a discussion of the necessity for building trade unions or an estimation of their importance. This lack undoubtedly was felt by the factory workers.

Along with this lack went the assumption that women possessed no political capacities. As a result the movement left untouched one of the most energizing factors which might have been brought into play to strengthen it. Here again, however, is demonstrated the limitations of the period rather than the limitations of the workers themselves.

Another weakness, resulting from the relationship of existing class forces, was the lax control exercised by the parties over the membership. Party membership apparently did not involve dues or similar obligations, but merely adherence to general principles. While this situation does not reflect on the loyalty of the members, it nevertheless prevented any great degree of party organization. This defect hindered building a solid body of adherents. The various conflicts scattered party forces.

The weaknesses of the movement, however, should not obscure its successes. Not only did the workers' political parties involve a large number of people but they also stimulated them to independent action, free of the parties of wealth and reaction.

Failure of the New York movement to live and expand is in general to be explained by the same reasons which brought about failure of the Philadelphia and other movements. Added to these, however, was internal discord, which sapped its vitality and turned its attention from the central task of building the party on a solid working class foundation. At bottom, the class character of the movement was not sufficiently conclusive to overcome the effects of dissension, and to insist upon strict adherence to issues of which the movement was an expression. As experience everywhere proved, getting workers into the movement was by no means difficult; there were real issues upon which they were willing to organize and fight. Throughout the state what was needed was decisive leadership, which only the New York City party could give, due to the industrial position of the city. When this example was not forthcoming, the movement in other localities fell apart or became corrupted by alliances with the old parties.

51

Although the political phase passed out of the foreground in 1834, nevertheless the workers' movement was left enormously strengthened. Spurred on by their experiences, the workers built more unions and waged many strikes for the shorter working day and for increased pay. In the years from 1791 to 1825, the 12 to 13-hour day prevailed in all industry; by 1840 the average was 11.4 hours a day; and, as a result of union pressure, the 10-hour day was established on all government works by President Martin Van Buren in an executive order of March 31, 1840. The first national union organization, the National Trades' Union, was born in 1834; it was the forerunner of the National Labor Union of 1866, of which William H. Sylvis was the head.[48]

The workers of one hundred years ago advanced to the limits of their capabilities. They even forged the rudiments of international working class solidarity, when Philadelphia workers staged a mass meeting to honor the workers of Paris for their part "in the recent glorious triumph of civil and religious liberty in France." [49]

The Jacksonian era is often referred to as "coonskin democracy" because of its frontier character and its leveling philosophy. Sharing with the frontier in giving substance to Jacksonianism, however, were the organized workmen of the East; they, together with the small farmer, formed the backbone of democracy.

Jackson's fight against monopoly and the Bank of the United States drew its staunchest support from both groups. Although their parties disappeared, the workers were far from being in a political slumber; a group in the former New York City party organized the Locofoco (workingmen's) movement within the Democratic party and elected one of their own number, Ely Moore, to Congress where he sat as the first labor representative in our history. In other sections of the East, where political action had coalesced into party forms, workingmen threw their support to Jackson.

The workingmen's movement gave life and substance to democracy and leavened the whole political life of the nation. The parties, though small and ineffective from today's viewpoint, must be reckoned a tremendous achievement of a labor movement which itself was only beginning to walk. And even in this stage, it recognized that trade unionism without political action was useless to advance the interests of its membership.

This is a great heritage for American labor in these days when the war is posing problems that go far beyond pure and simple trade unionism. The war is making politics the inescapable concern of all Americans. The question of whether labor should undertake political action is scarcely debatable. Politics is being thrust onto the unions, and every day it becomes clearer that the price of delay is exactly the same price workers would pay for leaving the conduct of any union affair in the hands of a local Chamber of Commerce.

History, that is good history, is never a study of the past for its own sake, but it is a guide to illuminate the present. The story of the first labor parties in America should enlighten our efforts today. The reasons which the workers gave one hundred years ago for action, their analysis of the economic, political, and social relationships in America form a background against which action can effectively be taken today.

The experiences of one hundred years ago, of course, cannot be copied in detail. But labor can study them and take them into account as it asserts itself as a political force. These experiences are a great heritage, a heritage which gathers force and significance as it is put to work by a modern labor movement in the interests of the nation as a whole.

REFERENCE NOTES

[1] *The New York Times*, Nov. 2, 1835. These figures were compiled in a special city census (not including Brooklyn), which disclosed a population of 269,873, whereof 43,091 were voters. *Cyclopedia of Political Review*, Vol. III, p. 853 quoted in *The American Historical Review*, Vol. XXIV, p. 396.

[2] John R. Commons and others, *Documentary History of American Industrial Society*, Vol. VI, p. 191, 1910.

[3] A. B. Darling, *Political Changes in Massachusetts, 1824-48*, p. 2, 1925. Many unskilled textile workers were recruited from among Irish immigrants, as were many of the railroad workers.

[4] F. J. Turner, *United States, 1830-50*, p. 102, 1935. In the South Atlantic, North Central and South Central, the respective figures for 1850 are 2 per cent, 2 per cent and 1 per cent.

[5] A Massachusetts Legislative report showed that children worked twelve and fifteen hours a day in most of the incorporated textile mills of the state. Massachusetts Legislative Files, 1825, Senate, No. 8074.

[6] *The Co-operator*, New York, Apr. 3, 1832.

[7] H. S. Zahler, *Eastern Workingmen and National Land Policy, 1829-1862*, 1942. This book provides an excellent summary of the work of Evans and National Reform, although the author's interpretative passages reflect a non-progressive school of economics.

[8] *Working Man's Advocate*, New York, Mar. 6, 1830. The report, "after much deliberation and some amendments made," was unanimously adopted at a meeting of the "friends of general and equal education" after consideration for three evenings, February 4, 8, and 11, 1830.

[9] Of the country's population 4.9 per cent lived in cities in 1820 and 6.7 per cent in 1830. U. S. Census, 1910, *Population* I, Table 33, p. 54.

[10] *Mechanics' Free Press*, June 21, 1828. No copies of the original pamphlet seem to have been preserved. It is interesting to note that its popularity was apparently responsible for its publication in the *Free Press* over a year after it was first issued.

[11] *Mechanics' Free Press*, Oct. 25, 1828. For some reason the preamble was not published until almost a year after its adoption, although its contents were widely known to the membership of the Association and of the unions which comprised it.

[12] *Mechanics' Free Press*, May 31, 1828.

[13] *Ibid.*, July 5, 1828.

[14] *Ibid.*, Sept. 27, 1828.

[15] Published in *Mechanics' Free Press*, Aug. 16, 1828.

[16] A special meeting of "the workingmen of Manyunk and its Vicinity" (now Manayunk)—a section of Philadelphia—endorsed the 1828 ticket, and appointed ten men as a vigilance committee. Earlier the county convention named its committee of 129 persons. *Mechanics' Free Press*, Oct. 11, 1828.

[17] *Mechanics' Free Press*, Nov. 1, 1828, printed an article on the duties of working class political clubs, suggesting, in addition to diffusion of information that funds be raised to print and circulate laws "and other important information," list all public offices, terms and salaries, establish free legal clinics for poor people, and secure public appropriations for these and other purposes.

[18] *Mechanics' Free Press*, Oct. 10, 1829.

[19] *Mechanics' Free Press*, Oct. 10, 1829. Previously, the city convention had agreed to refuse communications from either party (*Ibid.*, Sept. 12, 1829), and at the height of the election campaign, the Association issued a statement, declaring " . . . the workingmen disclaim any intention of aiding one of the political parties in preference to the other." (*Ibid.*, Oct. 3, 1829.)

[20] *Mechanics' Free Press*, Oct. 31, 1829.

[21] The address itself was devoted largely to discussion of the demand for a system of general education. Other programmatic points included reform of the banking system, abolition of compulsory militia service, public lotteries and imprisonment for debt, and reduction of property qualifications for public office holders. All of these issues, of course, were of statewide concern. *Mechanics' Free Press*, July 10, 1830.

[22] County conventions of the Democrats and Federalists in 1830 consisted of 26 delegates each.

[23] *Delaware Free Press*, July 31, 1830.

[24] April 16, 1831. The paper later passed into other hands, and reappeared in 1836 as the *National Labourer*, a trade union paper.

[25] An editorial in the *Mechanics' Free Press*, Apr. 16, 1831, listed the chief demands of the Philadelphia movement as "universal education, abolition of chartered monopolies, equal taxation, revision or abolition of militia system, all officers to be directly elected by the people, a less expensive law system, a lien law for laborers, no legislation on religion."

[26] These newspapers appeared in some 15 states between 1829 and 1832.

Some of them were not organs of any political party or association but advocated the principles of the workingman's political movement in a general way. States where papers existed were: Massachusetts, Maine, Vermont, Rhode Island, Connecticut, New York, Pennsylvania, New Jersey, Delaware, Maryland, Virginia, South Carolina, Ohio, Indiana, and Missouri.

[27] Quoted by Commons, *op. cit.*, p. 238.

[28] V. I. Lenin, *Selected Works*, Vol. XII, p. 302, 1938.

[29] From its resemblance to Thomas Paine's "Agrarian Justice," Skidmore's program became known as Agrarianism; he also derived many of his ideas from Thomas Spence and the latter's periodical *Pig's Meat*, London, 1794. For an elaboration of Spence's ideas, see Olive D. Udkin, *Thomas Spence and His Connections,* 1927.

[30] *Working Man's Advocate,* June 19, 1830.

[31] *Ibid.*

[32] *Ibid.*

[33] Chief among complaints of the party was the *Albany Regency*—a political machine—and the tight control exercised over selection of legislators by old party politicians; they came, of course, from the wealthy classes, "thereby leaving our own most numerous body without a voice in making those laws which we are compelled to obey," typically said *Working Man's Advocate,* Jan. 16, 1830.

[34] *Working Man's Advocate,* Jan. 2, 1830.

[35] *Ibid.,* Mar. 13, 1830.

[36] *Ibid.,* Mar. 20, 1830. The exception was the broker. As may be gathered, definition of a workingman was extremely broad.

[37] *Ibid.,* May 29, 1830.

[38] The original committee split 41-23 on the adoption of the majority report. John R. Commons and others, *History of Labour in the United States,* p. 257.

[39] Party newspapers in these cities opposed state guardianship, playing down, however, the majority charges of "infidelity," and basing their position on the plan's impracticability. Newspapers of Buffalo and Genesee, the latter under the editorship of Orestes Brownson, approved Owen's proposal.

[40] *Free Enquirer,* New York, Oct. 7, 1829.

[41] Mathews Cary, *Select Excerpta,* Vol. XXI, pp. 156-60.

[42] Seth Luther, one of the earliest agitators against child labor, said in his "Address to the Working Men of New England," that mill owners "go into the shop of the Carpenter, and others who carry on business, and actually *forbid* them to employ what they sneeringly call 'ten hour men.'"

Quoted by John R. Commons and others, *History of Labour in the United States*, Vol. I, p. 325.

[43] Carey, *op. cit.*, Vol. IV, p. 435.

[44] *Ibid*.

[45] *Free Enquirer*, Sept. 22, 1832.

[46] Quoted by John R. Commons and others, *History of Labour in the United States*, Vol. I, p. 314.

[47] John R. Commons and others, *History of Labour in the United States*, Vol. I, pp. 215-16.

[48] For an extensive account of the struggles for shorter working hours, see Labor Research Association, *The History of the Shorter Workday*, 1942; for an account of Sylvis, see Charlotte Todes, *William H. Sylvis and the National Labor Union*, 1942.

[49] *Mechanics' Free Press*, Oct. 2, 1830. The Revolution of 1830 failed to gain the triumph hoped for by the Philadelphia workers, for the monarchy of Louis Phillipe quickly suppressed the revolution, and with it civil and religious liberty.

PLATFORM AND RESOLUTIONS OF
NEW YORK WORKING MEN'S PARTY*

DEMANDS DEALING WITH PUBLIC SCHOOLS, LIEN LAW, IMPRISON-
MENT FOR DEBT, THE NATIONAL BANK, REFORM OF COURTS, ETC.

We take this opportunity solemnly to aver, whatever may be said to the contrary by ignorant or designing individuals, or biased presses, that we have no desire or intention of disturbing the rights of property in individuals, or the public. On the contrary, we consider the acquiring of property to soften the asperities of sickness, of age, and for the benefit of our posterity, as one of the greatest incentives to industry. . . .

Another object for which we contend, in which we claim from our sectional and state legislatures as a right, is the appropriation of our public funds to a reasonable extent, for the purpose of education, upon a system that shall enable all before the age of twenty-one, to acquire a competent knowledge of the language of their country, arithmetic, geography, history, natural philosophy, geometry and chemistry, as applied to the arts. A system that shall unite under the same roof the children of the poor man and the rich, the widow's charge and the orphan, where the road to distinction shall be superior industry, virtue and acquirements, without reference to descent.

We believe that our existing system of education, if continued, under which many are deprived of all or nearly all its advantages, and which tends in a greater or less degree to separate the children of the poor man and the rich, will eventually lead us into all the

* Abridged text of address and resolutions of the conference committee of New York wards. From a pamphlet entitled, *Proceedings of a Meeting of Mechanics and other Working Men, held at Military Hall, Wooster Street, New York, on Tuesday evening, Dec. 29, 1829.* (New York, 1830.)

distinctions that exist under despotic governments, and destroy our political liberties. We ask if many of the monopolists and aristocrats in our city would not consider it disgraceful to their noble children to have them placed in our public schools by the side of the children of the poor yet industrious mechanics; and has not this same feeling extended to a considerable degree already throughout the country? We believe, that as a nation or state, the first subject which should engross our attention, or for which the public funds should be appropriated, is education. When this shall have been effectually attended to, we will cheerfully unite in support of any other just and feasible object. But we do not believe in the right of our legislators to appropriate public funds for the endowment of colleges and academies, almost solely for the benefit of the rich, while our primary schools have but to a limited extent secured the advantages even of a partial education to the producing classes of the community.

We ask of our state legislature the passage of a Lien Law for the security of every individual who shall furnish either labor or materials towards the erection, completion or necessary repairs of any building. This we demand, that a large portion of our citizens may be as truly secured in their rights, as their more wealthy, but not more worthy, neighbors. That the many hardships we endure, and disadvantages we have labored under, have not been so sensibly felt by the mechanics of the country, is no doubt true. Their situation and ours is materially different; the standing and ability of individuals for whom they labor are more generally known, or easily ascertained, by them, than with us.

The farmers by whom they are principally employed are the most industrious, the most virtuous, and all things considered, the most intelligent portion of men in this or any other country; possessing, as yet, the majority, their rights have been less openly invaded by wealthy or designing politicians. The evils of which we complain, if not immediately redressed, will shortly become equally burdensome and grievous to them. . . .

They need but be told that many of our buildings are erected by designing speculators, or master builders, who, when detected, are regularly succeeded by others—that a systematic course of frauds has been practised on the mechanics, laborers, and furnishers of materials for buildings, for years, in this city, to the amount of $125,000 annually. That the greater part of these losses have fallen upon individuals who have families dependent on their labor for support. That the merchant who vends his merchandise can secure payment, previous to delivery, while the mechanic and producing classes are obliged to fulfil their contracts, or render their services before they can demand such security. That a great part of the distress, experienced in this city during the last winter, originated in these losses. That we are now, from the same causes, looking forward with fearful forebodings to the events of the present winter.

The farmers need but be truly informed of these facts, to unite with one accord in the passage of a lien law, which would protect us, hereafter, from many otherwise unavoidable evils.

RESOLUTIONS

RESOLVED, that we should be unjust to ourselves, to our posterity and the public, were we to suffer the vile slanders that have been unjustly heaped upon us by ignorant and biased individuals and presses to pass unnoticed.

RESOLVED, that we explicitly disavow all intentions to intermeddle with the rights of individuals, either as to property or religion; but that we hold these rights as sacred as life, not to be approached by ruthless despots or visionary fanatics.

RESOLVED, that it is wholly incompatible with human rights that any free citizen, who has duly surrendered all his property to his creditors, should for one moment be deprived of his liberty.

RESOLVED, that we are in favor of searching laws, for the detection of concealed or fraudulently conveyed property, and emphatically in favor of the entire abolishment of imprisonment for debts.

RESOLVED, that it is the earnest wish of this meeting, that our representatives in the next legislature, early in the session, introduce and support a bill for the abolishment of imprisonment for debt.

RESOLVED, that next to life and liberty we consider education the greatest blessing bestowed on mankind.

RESOLVED, that the public funds should be appropriated (to a reasonable extent) to the purposes of education, upon a regular system, that shall ensure the opportunity to every individual of obtaining a competent education before he shall have arrived at the age of maturity.

RESOLVED, that the banks, under the administration of their present directors and officers ... form a monopoly that is hostile to the equal rights of the American merchant, manufacturer, mechanic, and laboring man; and that the renewal, by the legislature, of the charters prayed for, will confirm and perpetuate an aristocracy, which eventually may shake the foundations of our liberties, and entail slavery on our posterity.

RESOLVED, that our post office has not been located with an eye to the general interest and rapid growth of the city, and consequently subjects the laboring classes of the community to great inconveniences; and it should be immediately removed to the most central part of the city.

RESOLVED, that our courts of justice should be so reformed, that the producing classes may be placed on an equality with the wealthy.

RESOLVED, that as faithful sentinels we will guard the temple of our liberties and all further encroachments; that united we shall keep the field, and maintain the war, until the justice of our demands shall be fully disseminated throughout the United States, the lost ground regained, and our principles established upon an unchangeable basis.

LIST OF LABOR PARTIES

The following is a list of independent workers' political parties organized in 61 cities and towns during 1827-1834:

CONNECTICUT: Lyme, New Haven, New London

DELAWARE: Wilmington

MAINE: Portland, Saco

MASSACHUSETTS: Boston, Cambridge, Charlestown, Dedham, Dorchester, Lowell, New Bedford, Northampton, Plymouth, Waltham

NEW HAMPSHIRE: Dover

NEW JERSEY: Newark, Trenton

NEW YORK: Albany, Auburn, Batavia, Brockport, Brooklyn, Buffalo, Canandaigua, Genesee, Geneva, Glens' Falls, Ithaca, Kingsbury, Lansingburgh, New York, Palmyra, Rochester, Saratoga, Schenectady, Syracuse, Troy, Utica

OHIO: Canton, Cincinnati, Columbian County, Zanesville

PENNSYLVANIA: Carlisle, Clearfield, Erie, Harrisburg, Lancaster, Milesburg, Philadelphia, Phillipsburg, Pike Township, Pittsburgh, Pottsville

RHODE ISLAND: Providence

WASHINGTON, D.C.

VERMONT: Burlington, Calais, Middlebury, Woodstock

SELECTED BIBLIOGRAPHY

Beard, Charles A. and Mary R. *The Rise of American Civilization,* Ch. XII. Macmillan, 1930.

Carey, Mathew. *Select Excerpta.* Mss., New York Public Library.

Commons, John R., and others. *Documentary History of American Industrial Society,* Vol. V, Macmillan, 1910.
History of Labour in the United States, Vol. I, Macmillan, 1918.

Darling, A. B. *Political Changes in Massachusetts, 1824-48.* 1925.

Evans, George Henry. *History of the Workingmen's Party.* New York, 1842.

Labor Research Association. *The History of the Shorter Workday.* International, 1942.

Mechanics' Free Press, Philadelphia Public Library.

Morison, Samuel and Henry Steele Commager. *The Growth of the American Republic, 1865-1937,* Vol. I, Chs. XXIII, XXV. Third edition. Revised. Oxford, 1942.

Myers, Gustavus. *History of Tammany Hall.* Macmillan, 1901.

Pancoast, Elinor, and Anne E. Lincoln. *The Incorrigible Idealist: Robert Dale Owen in America.* Principia Press, 1940.

Perkins, A.J.G., and Theresa Wolfson. *Frances Wright, Free Enquirer.* Harper, 1939.

Rudkin, Olive D. *Thomas Spence and His Connections.* International, 1927.

Skidmore, Thomas. *The Rights of Man to Property: Being a proposition to make it equal among the Adults of the Present Generation; and to Provide for its Equal Transmission to Every Individual of Each Succeeding Generation, on arriving at the Age of Maturity.* New York, 1829.

Todes, Charlotte. *William H. Sylvis and the National Labor Union.* International, 1942.

Workingmen's Advocate, New York Public Library.

Zahler, H.S. *Eastern Workingmen and National Land Reform, 1829-1862.* Columbia, 1942.